TRAUMA HEALING JOURNAL

This Journal is dedicated to all those who have experienced trauma from abuse or other circumstances. You endure a silent struggle but you are not alone. I truly wish you happiness and healing and I hope that this journal helps you in some way.

YOU ARE FEARFULLY AND WONDERFULLY MADE.

DIFFICULT ROADS OFTEN LEAD TO BEAUTIFUL DESTINATIONS

Welcome to your healing journal.

In this journal, you will find writing prompts to encourage deep thinking about how your past has affected you and how you can overcome your obstacles.

This journal is for you and you alone.
No one else can feel what you are feeling. Be open and honest with yourself. Dig deep within to find your true answers. This is your safe space. In the end of this book, you will also find ideas for self-care and positive affirmations to help you on your journey to greatness. Your past does not define your future.

This journal should help you to become mindful of your emotions and expand your self-awareness. Shift your mindset and defeat your fears. What will you do to improve your future and be the best version of yourself?

No matter how bad my day is, these 10 things always make me feel better:

_____

_____

_____

_____

_____

_____

_____

_____

_____

_____

_____

_____

_____

_____

_____

_____

_____

_____

the flower
that blooms
in adversity
is the most rare
and beautiful
of all.

- MULAN

The greatest challenge in my life right now is

What are the three things that scare you the most and why?

what we
don't need in
the midst of
struggle is
shame for
being human.

- BRENE BROWN

Do you have any recurring dreams?

Is there anything you're scared to admit out loud?

YOU DON'T
HAVE TO HAVE
IT ALL
FIGURED OUT
TO MOVE
FORWARD...
JUST TAKE
THE NEXT
STEP.

Unknown

Write about a difficult time in your life that you overcame and how you overcame it

When was the last time you cried?

SOMETIMES COURAGE IS

THE QUIET VOICE AT THE

END OF THE DAY SAYING

"I WILL TRY AGAIN TOMORROW"

MARY ANNE RADMACHER

What is your favourite way to express yourself?

What methods do you use for coping?

You're a
warrior.
Warriors
don't give up
and they don't
back down.
Pick up your
sword and
shield and
fight.

- BODHI SANDERS

Do you have a support team? If so, who are they? If not, what steps will you take to build a strong support system?

_____

_____

_____

_____

_____

_____

_____

_____

_____

_____

_____

_____

_____

_____

_____

_____

_____

_____

_____

When you think of what you're going through, what fears come to mind?

You are not
a victim.
Just a
fighter with
scars that
few can
understand.

- LZ

Do you find it easy or difficult to express your true feelings? Why?

_____

_____

_____

_____

_____

_____

_____

_____

_____

_____

_____

_____

_____

_____

_____

_____

_____

What triggers are affecting you?

stay patient and trust your journey

Why have you decided to face your abuse or trauma now?

_____

_____

_____

_____

_____

_____

_____

_____

_____

_____

_____

_____

_____

_____

_____

_____

_____

_____

_____

What has your fear stopped you from doing?

She remembered who she was and the game changed.

- LALAH DELIAH

What do you want to achieve by facing your trauma?

Is the trauma still affecting you? How so?

Life is tough,
my darling,
but so are you.

- STEPHANIE BENNETT HENRY

In order to move forward, you must forgive yourself.
Have you forgiven yourself?

_____

_____

_____

_____

_____

_____

_____

_____

_____

_____

_____

_____

_____

_____

_____

_____

_____

What is your plan to escape the trauma and abuse?

_____

_____

_____

_____

_____

_____

_____

_____

_____

_____

_____

_____

_____

_____

_____

_____

_____

_____

_____

The comeback
is always
stronger than
the setback

How could you use your situation to help others?

Write a list of reasons why you deserve better?

Nothing can dim the light that shines from within.

- MAYA ANGELOU

How do you let negative feelings affect you?

How can you become a thriver rather than a victim?

Stay positive even when it feels like your whole world is falling apart.

- ANONYMOUS

Define who you are based on self-love and your real self-worth.

_____

_____

_____

_____

_____

_____

_____

_____

_____

_____

_____

_____

_____

_____

_____

_____

_____

_____

_____

_____

She was powerful,
not because she
wasn't scared but
because she went
on so strongly,
despite the fear.

- ATTICUS

Do you allow hurtful things other people say to affect you?

What advice would you give to your childhood self?

I can and I will. watch me.

- CARRIE GREEN

Go back to your fears and redefine them.

How does it feel to be the age you currently are?

If there's one thing I'm willing to bet on, it's myself.

- BEYONCE

Describe the type of person you aspire to be.

How can you become that strong person you aspire to be?

She's everything,
even when she's
treated like
nothing.

- R.H. SIN

What is your greatest obstacle right now?

What steps can you take to remove this obstacle? How can you overcome it?

_____

_____

_____

_____

_____

_____

_____

_____

_____

_____

_____

_____

_____

_____

_____

_____

_____

_____

You are braver
than you believe,
stronger than
you seem,
smarter than
you think.

What are 5 goals you have for your future?

Name 5 things you love about yourself

She looked back on
her life and
realized that
everything that
happened only
made her
stronger.

Do you find yourself being more negative than positive?

What could you do to change your outlook on life?

I survived because the fire inside me burned brighter than the fire around me.

- JOSHUA GRAHAM

When is the last time you felt joy?

How do you feel right now compared to a year ago?

_____

_____

_____

_____

_____

_____

_____

_____

_____

_____

_____

_____

_____

_____

_____

_____

you are
powerful,
beautiful,
brilliant and
brave.

What makes you feel alive?

When do you feel most successful?

SHE'S BEEN THROUGH HELL AND CAME OUT AN ANGEL. YOU DIDN'T BREAK HER, DARLING. YOU DON'T OWN THAT KIND OF POWER.

- BMM POETRY

What 5 things are you most grateful for and why?

Where is your "happy place"?

You are fierce.
You're a survivor.
You're a fighter
through and
through.
Little brave, breathe.
There is a warrior
within you.

- BEAU TAPLIN

How do you handle stressful situations?

What is one thing you can do each day to improve your mental health?

_____

_____

_____

_____

_____

_____

_____

_____

_____

_____

_____

_____

_____

_____

_____

_____

You are fierce.
You are more
powerful than
you know; you
are beautiful
just as you are.

- MELISSA ETHERIDGE

How have your struggles made you stronger or weaker?

_____

_____

_____

_____

_____

_____

_____

_____

_____

_____

_____

_____

_____

_____

_____

_____

_____

_____

What lessons have you learned?

You are fierce.
It took me quite a
long time to develop
a voice and now
that I have it, I
am not going to
be silent.

- MADELEINE ALBRIGHT

What are your regrets?

_____

_____

_____

_____

_____

_____

_____

_____

_____

_____

_____

_____

_____

_____

_____

_____

_____

YOU
ARE
GETTING
STRONGER
EVERY
DAY

What are you most proud of and why?

It's okay to be a glowstick. Sometimes we need to break before we can shine.

UNKNOWN

What are 5 things you can do to improve your life?

_____

_____

_____

_____

_____

_____

_____

_____

_____

_____

_____

_____

_____

_____

_____

_____

_____

_____

Self-Care Healing Ideas

Go for a walk

Meditate

Journal

Yoga

Read a book

Take a nap

Dance like no one's watching

Social Media detox

Listen to happy music & sing

Keep a gratitude journal

Spend time with a friend

Take a long bubble bath

Eat a sweet treat

Listen to a podcast

Enjoy a sunrise or sunset

Affirmations

I am enough

I tried my best today

MY POSSIBILITIES ARE ENDLESS

I am worthy

I can achieve my goals

I love myself

Negativity will not affect me

I deserve the very best

I am beautiful

I AM BRAVE AND STRONG

I will be kind to others

My struggle does not define me

I am safe

I will focus on the positive

I forgive myself for my wrongs

Made in United States
Troutdale, OR
10/18/2023

13805128R00060